Chasing the Empire

Our Journey Towards Legacy and Love

BY

David & Jessica Martin

DEDICATION

This book is dedicated to our children who inspire us to build an empire and leave a legacy. To our parents who paved the way and the many people that we have been called to serve through the credit repair and legacy building process.

This is for you!

ACKNOWLEDGMENTS

JESSICA,

To my children Jaria, Lamariyah, D'heiress, thank you for growing with me along the way. You were my inspiration to never give up. You watched me grow and you grew with me.

To my coaches; Kristy Jackson, thanks for taking me under your wings and giving me a chance when no 'one else would; Derrick Harper who helped me to build a better business, & Stormy Wellington for helping me understand that I was worthy of being wealthy and for helping me expand my mindset.

To my grandparents Rob & Jessie Ellis, Thanks for instilling the word of God in me, for always being there for me and teaching me to always put God first.

To my sisters and brothers, I want to encourage you to always put God first no matter what, to always live your best life. Stay encouraged even when life gets hard. Don't ever lose sight of your potential. You deserve the empire. Build it and God will bless it.

DAVID,

To my brother James Martin Jr. "Boo" and his wife, Cindy for being a healthy example of lasting love.

To my children for always keeping me young and motivated. You are my fuel and I love you dearly. To my parents for always believing that I would a star.

To my close friends, Max Wells, Lashaun Glover, Andrew Curbin, Antoine Burkes who held me down during hard times and stayed solid during my hard moments. They helped me hold down the fort during my wife's incarceration. Your support was invaluable.

To Brandon Sneed, for your unrelenting support. You are one of my closest friend and I'm grateful for our brotherhood.

TABLE OF CONTENTS

ᴜᴜᴜᴜᴜᴜᴜᴜᴜᴜᴜᴜᴜᴜᴜᴜᴜᴜᴜᴜᴜᴜᴜᴜᴜᴜᴜᴜ

INTRODUCTION

*"You will know that you are the chosen
one when the odds are stacked against you and
you succeed anyway"*

~SRJ

*"When you're not born into legacy,
you must create one."*

When you come from the bottom, success is about survival. It's about bouncing back from the things that were supposed to break you. Success is about failing along the way because your path is made of challenges that have been designed to test you, yet make you better. It's about deciding that you want more out of life, and then getting up every day "No Matter What" and working towards it. Success for survivors is simple, you have to make it! You must overcome the many obstacles that rise up against you, because if not you, then who? When no one before you has paved a path, or left behind a plan, you find yourself building without a blueprint. You're forced to learn and even suffer as the result of the knowledge you don't have and the resources you don't have access to. Too often, the members of our communities become the recipients of debt, trauma and a cycle of poverty, but I knew that I would do something different. I wanted to see the people around me make it and I was willing to risk it all to make it happen.

When people look at our lives now, we want them to be inspired, but more than anything, we want them to know that they have the power to be the difference in their families. There's a saying that, "If you don't come from a rich family, a rich family must come from you," this is something that we live by. To be honest, all we ever wanted to do was be able to provide for our families, and escape the trenches of the inner city. On our journey we have lost and we have learned a lot, but we never gave up. Truthfully, we couldn't afford to. We had so many people depending on us, so even when we were down to nothing, we kept pushing forward. We kept going while carrying the weight of grief, and the frustration that comes with just trying to get by. We were bold enough to have a vision for ourselves that was bigger than anything we'd ever been exposed to. We had experienced our share of pain, trouble, struggle, and setbacks, but we had dreams of building an empire and we bonded over it.

They say, "a woman's loyalty is tested when her man has nothing, and a man's loyalty is tested when he has everything." It's about remembering the bond when life brings you to a breaking point, and staying committed until you reach a breakthrough. When I first met David as I was walking out of a gas station in Houston Texas, I had no idea that he would become the love of my life, or that he would prove the true strength of a real bond. Our wedding ceremony was a beautiful experience that will always be remembered as the moment that changed the trajectory of our lives. Most people feel this was after they say, "I Do", but for me it was deeper than that. The day after we exchanged vows, the man who had received me as his lawfully wedded wife would now have to drive me to the correctional facility where I had to turn myself in to serve a 6 -month prison sentence. I can only imagine how difficult it had to be for him to raise our girls, maintain our life and encourage me while I was behind bars, but he did it.

It was during my time incarcerated that I discovered purpose. I found myself helping the women I was locked up with to understand and build their credit. I knew that if they had financial literacy tools and strategies, they could have a fresh start when they got out. I developed an interest in teaching them things I had learned the hard way. It's so easy to lose hope when you're isolated from those you love, but I knew that I couldn't dwell on that. Helping my fellow inmates was also helping me to discover a passion for empowering women to develop profit strategies that would help them build generational wealth. Plus, I was no longer willing to risk time away from my family so I decided to legitimize my hustle.

Being released from prison was like breaking free from a cocoon and spreading my wings. Just like a butterfly, my season of isolation gave me an opportunity to experience transformation. After returning home to my family, my focus was different and my ambition was in overdrive. I used a lot of my time locked up thinking, dreaming and planning. So, when I got home, I was clear about what I wanted and what it would take to get there. I had to become the woman that could nurture a marriage, raise babies and build a business the legal way.

My husband taught me the power of partnerships. I'm so happy that I had him on my side during one of the most challenging times in my life. What I realized is that, when it comes to partnerships, the key is choosing someone you can grow with and nurturing a bond with those you can build with.

It's ironic how the hardest times in our lives give us the most strength. I've learned lessons from my losses, and the things that were supposed to break me only made me better. I'm not saying this to glorify or glamorize pain and struggle. In fact, I wrote this book to inspire you to break the chains in your own family. I believe that the work we do and the legacy we leave behind should set our children up to succeed. When we create a strong foundation, and we impart wisdom and wealth strategies into our children, their success can be defined by thriving and not just surviving.

Chasing the Empire is more than another self-help book. In this book we share our stories in raw form. It's easy to look at our lives now and applaud our accolades, but what about the days when we were broke, exhausted, confused, frustrated, incarcerated and overwhelmed. Those were the moments when we had to keep working even when no one was clapping. Those were the times that developed our character, revealed our resilience and strengthened our bond. It's our stories that make us who we are, and it's the legacy we are working to leave behind for our children that fuel us. In this book we share our stories with transparency and authenticity. As you peel back each page, you will gain insight on the mindset, business principles, wealth building strategies, family philosophy and faith values that have contributed to our growth.

This book was written for the go-getters who have to get it out of the mud. For the chosen ones who have to be the first to do something different in their families. This book is for those who refuse to settle for what society says they can have because they believe that God has a Good plan for their lives.... even if it gets hard along the way. This book is about building, growing, learning, leading and leaving a legacy. This book is for those who have hustle in their heart and wake up with the grind on their mind. This book is for the young, black and gifted who believe that they can go higher....for the resilient ones who are bold enough to step into the fire and are relentlessly *Chasing the Empire*.

PART ONE

THE BEGINNING OF
AN UNBREAKABLE BOND

"Our Love Story"

> *"The greatest action of love is unrelenting loyalty during the times that test you the most. It takes a strong bond to hit rock bottom with a person and instead of breaking, you start to build"*
> **~David and Jessica Martin**

I t all started at a gas station in Houston. I was making a quick stop for gas and blunts when David approached me. He asked me my name and where I was from. This is when we realized that we were both from Chicago. I ended up giving him my number and he called me right away. He seemed like a cool guy, but I wasn't looking for a relationship. I was a single mother of two and doing well on my own. During that time, 'I was making about five thousand dollars a week helping my clients overcome housing challenges. I was in a good place financially; my focus at that time, was reserved for activities that helped me to increase my funds and my family. Although I wasn't looking for a relationship, there was something about David that intrigued me so, I gave him my number. It didn't take long for him to call. Whenever I would talk to him, I would notice more and more how much he reminded me of myself. He was ambitious and he was driven to make it by any means necessary.

We would talk on the phone often and I would buy weed from him from time to time. David was eager to get to know me better and would persistently ask me out on dates. I was focused on the many responsibilities that required my attention so I didn't have a lot of free time. Whenever he offered to take me out on a date, I would come up with an excuse to decline his requests. I don't know if it was his persistence or his character that made me decide to make time to take him up on his offer, But I was glad that I did.

Our first date was at a pool parlor in Spring, Texas. Not only did we have a lot in common, but we had really good chemistry together. Whenever we were together, it was like we had known one another our whole lives even though we had just met. I was so comfortable with him. I felt understood, seen and valued. He understood me in a way that never required me to say a word. I was able to understand him in that same way. I could tell that he was a hustler too. He had values, dreams and integrity. We started spending a lot of time together and we fell in love quickly. David had lost many of his loved ones. His brother was murdered the night of his graduation, his father not long after that and his mother passed away about a month before we met.

I understood what it was like to lose someone you loved and I admired his strength. Like me, he knew how to pick up the pieces and push forward, even with a broken heart. A part of me wanted to mend his broken pieces, and create a life of peace that we both deserved. It would take a lot of hard lessons before we would make the mental, inner and environmental changes required to experience a total life change; but we would eventually get there with grit and God's grace.

When David and I met, we were both in a season of survival. We were committed to getting what we needed in order to survive the moment. But, after we started getting serious in our relationship, we both wanted more than to survive the day, we wanted to build for the future. I understood the buying power of good credit, so naturally I checked his credit report. To my surprise, he had pretty good credit. His profile was free of debt outside of a three-hundred-dollar cable bill. I was able to dispute the collection and it was removed from his credit report.

I always thought David was a good catch and I didn't understand how the women before me let him get away. He was kind, yet strong. He had good credit, a bachelor's degree and was a member of a Kappa Alpha Psi Fraternity Incorporated. David's fraternal background imparted the importance of community and brotherhood into him. I was falling head over heels the more I got to know him and I was realizing more and more that he was someone I could build with. He possessed many qualities that I admired. He was strong in areas where I was weak, I matched his hustle and our ambitions were aligned. I had a vision for all the powerful and amazing things that we could do together. I was making good money before I met him, but he added fuel to my flame. He pushed me to take my hustle to the next level. He was well connected so my clientele increased once we combined forces. Together, we were both making more money.

I learned pretty quickly that money wasn't the only qualifier for success. I was making six figures off of multiple hustles and I was still making poor choices. I was sporting a designer bag full of cash and credit cards when I was caught shoplifting in Macy's. I had access to funds but I was still operating from a "broke mindset." It doesn't matter how much money you can get if you continue to think poor. I felt entitled to things that I had not earned. I was very selfish at that time. I never thought about how my actions would impact others. I only cared about what I could get. I didn't consider consequences because I simply didn't care.

It would take three strikes, a six-month prison sentence, a love that inspired me to dream of a better future and a rock bottom experience before I would finally change my mind and my life.

David and I were dating for a year before he proposed to me. Shortly after finding out that we were expecting our first child together, we were engaged. Our romance was on the fast track. We really fueled one another. Individually we were great, but together we were on another level. We had multiple streams on income. We were selling drugs, cars, and spending money on lavish items. We were making a lot of money and then spending it to look rich. In fact, we jokingly refer to ourselves as the "hood" version of the Obama's. It was one of the reasons we chose the Cultural Center as our wedding venue. This is where the Obama's had tied the knot. We were high off of life, living it up and spending a lot of money preparing for our lavish wedding ceremony. We considered ourselves presidential. We were going to live a good life one way or another.

Even our engagement party was a huge production. We rented out a mansion and flew family and friends out to celebrate with us.

We were having the time of our lives. It all came crashing down when I caught my third strike. It was six months until our wedding day, and I violated my probation by catching another case.

As if things couldn't get any worse, David was pulled over for a traffic violation as he was pulling out of the family dollar. He was on the way home with our daughter when she asked for a bag of Cheetos. He was pulled over as he was leaving the store. When the officer ran his driver's license, it was determined that David had a warrant for his arrest in St. Louis. The warrant was issued as a result of a "failure to appear." The court hearing was associated with his drug trafficking case. He was unaware of the hearing and was shocked when he was arrested and transported back to St. Louis. He didn't receive a bond so he wasn't able to get out right away.

We knew that we needed to make some serious changes when were both in jail at the same time. The fast life came with consequences, sacrifice, loss and jail time.... and we were tired.

We were both eventually released on bond. We continued to move forward because the streets conditioned us to keep going. We were planning our wedding day while fighting court cases. My case would end in a plea deal to accept a felony charge and a prison sentence in exchange for permission to leave the state to attend our wedding. The system had me in a tight spot but I wasn't going to let anything stop me from marrying the love of my life.

I accepted my fate and I relied on faith to get me through it. I fell more in love with my husband when he stepped up to the plate and took such good care of our children and our home while I was away. Missing them was the hardest thing that I ever had to do. Once I was locked up, I was unable to communicate with my husband or children for over a month. Once I was finally able to schedule a visit, the facility canceled the visitation because Hurricane Harvey had hit Texas hard leaving the jail surrounded by floods and damaged phone towers. Every time I would cry, I would tell myself that I was never going to put myself or my family in this situation again. Missing them was the most excruciating pain that I had ever endured. With the additional delays caused by the storm, I was unable to see or communicate with my family for over three months.

I was living through a valley experience. Reaching rock bottom opened my eyes, changed my focus and introduced me to purpose. You don't expect to find purpose in prison, but there was something about being separated and isolated from everything I loved that made me begin to see new possibilities in life. I made plans to have a more positive future. I realized that purpose is discovered when you think about what you can do for other people. Even though I was behind bars, I didn't allow my skills to go to waste. As I taught the women who were locked up with me the proper and legal way to repair their credit on their own, the more I realized that I could actually make more money, scale my operations plus increase revenue by implementing all legitimate practices. Working with the women in prison kept my skills sharp and it birthed a passion for empowering women to build generational wealth through financial literacy, credit repair and healthy money management.

PART TWO

FEARS, TEARS
AND HARD TRUTHS
"Jessica's Journey"

"Do not judge me by my success, judge me
by how many times I fell down and still
pulled myself up again"
~Nelson Mandela

I remember it like it was yesterday. I was six years old and the youngest of my mother's children. My siblings and I were all dressed up and excited to meet our mother for the first time. The supervised visit was arranged to take place at my aunt's house. It felt like a true celebratory moment. I recall feeling a bit confused, yet curious. I had always believed that my father's girlfriend was my mother. It wasn't until we were told that a meeting had been set up for us to meet our biological mother when we realized, that the woman we had known up until that point, wasn't our actual mother. As my young mind tried to make sense of what was happening, a part of me looked forward to the meeting with childlike eagerness and anticipation.

When we arrived at my aunt's house, she had games set up in the backyard for us to play while we waited for our mother to arrive. The mesquite aroma of grilled barbeque filled the air and everyone seemed so elated. The moment she arrived; my eyes locked in on her. She was so beautiful and dressed in fancy clothing. She walked in with her husband and she was so proud to show us off to her family. As she swooned over us, I remember her smiling and telling me how pretty I was. She continued to hug us tightly as she smiled from ear to ear showering us with her love and affection.

Although I didn't know her, I remember feeling so loved and valued by her. Her energy was so inviting, and I was happy to meet and get to know her. Meeting my mother for the first time was a beautiful experience, unfortunately it would also be the last time I'd ever get to see her.

A few weeks later, my grandmother and my aunt showed up at our home in the projects. They came to break the news to my father about my mother. I knew something bad had happened because of the look on my father's face. He eventually approached my siblings and I as we sat around the kitchen table eating breakfast. He had another surprising message for us regarding our mother, only this time we were not only confused, but we were devastated. With reluctancy, he informed us that my mother had been killed in a car accident. I was in disbelief. I blurted out, "You mean that pretty lady that we just met?" I could tell that it was hard for my father to break the news to us. He nodded his head forward slowly, confirming my fears that the woman I had just been reunited with, had now passed away. It was so emotionally traumatizing that I ended up developing a phobia of cars. I was so afraid to drive and would experience anxiety while riding in motor vehicles. For this reason, I didn't get my driver's license until I was 21 years old, and even after obtaining my license, I still suffered through fear whenever I was in a car. At six years old, my young mind was now programmed to believe that cars could kill the beautiful people who loved you. This trauma has stuck with me over the years. Even as an adult, I still don't like to drive.

Throughout my childhood, I lived with the sad truth that a beautiful bond was cut short because of a tragic car accident. It wasn't until I became a rebellious teenager that I was able to unveil a more sinister truth. I was about sixteen years old when I started running away from home. My grandmother was raising me and I started to rebel against her strict rules. I wanted to do what I wanted to do, and I didn't want to take orders from anyone, so, I left. I would leave home to stay with various friends, cousins and other family members. It was during that time when I found out that the car accident my mother was involved in was much more diabolical and intentional than we originally believed. It turned out that a car was indeed involved in the incident, but it wasn't an accident at all. My mother was beaten to death and once she was unresponsive, she was dragged into the road where her body was driven over several times by a 3000-pound vehicle. She had been run over so severely that parts of her body were dismembered. When the detectives were unable to charge anyone with the crime, my mother's murder case eventually went cold. It wasn't until my sister began to place pressure on the investigators that they decided to take another look at her case. After over ten years, my mother's case was reopened. Her husband who had joined her to meet us for the first time was eventually charged with her murder. He was sentenced to life in prison where he eventually died while incarcerated in the year 2020.

My older sister had always believed that he was the culprit. She found out that he spent twenty-five years in prison for the murder of his first wife. He was convicted of beating her to death with a hammer in front of their children. Discovering the truth about my mother's murder was too heavy to fully process. I often wondered why my mother chose to marry a man who had been convicted of the murder of his first wife. At six years old, I remember my mother's husband sitting on the front row of her funeral. He appeared to be completely distraught. He was inconsolable as he cried out loudly in despair. As he wept uncontrollably, my older sister was being pulled out of the church. She was inconsolable as well. As my mother's husband cried out, my sister yelled out in anger and immense frustration. I remember her directing all of her pain and anger towards my mother's husband screaming, "you killed her, you killed my mother, I know you killed her!" We didn't know it at the time, but it turned out that my sister was right.

To be honest, I never shared the disturbing and graphic details of her brutal murder until I began the process of writing this book. I buried that information in the back of my mind. Since I had more questions than answers, it was easier to push it out of my mind rather than processing the pain of the gruesome truth. I had never even shared the details with my husband. He knew that the car accident turned out to not have been an accident at all, but the diabolical details were never discussed until I decided to write and release this book.

My fear of driving in cars transformed into a reluctance to get married or even commit in a relationship. How could the person who vowed to love you take your life away in such a malicious manner?

My evolution into womanhood was a very rocky one. I suffered with low self-esteem, a lack of self-worth and I had no sense of direction. The one thing I had always been good at was making money, but with no real guidance, role models or mentors, I was reckless, promiscuous, and headed down a path of self-destruction. Eventually my choices led me into becoming a teen mother. Raising a daughter without a real blueprint for proper parenting challenged me at my core. I loved my daughter deeply, but I didn't have the tools at the time to be the example that she deserved. I was an alcoholic high school drop out that spent my time engaging in various criminal activities to make money. I was addicted to fast money and I was really good at getting it. At 16 years old, I was raising a baby on my own. By the time I turned 17, I was sleeping on floors with my baby at my cousins apartment. As if sleeping on the floor wasn't hard enough, when my cousins boyfriend was released from jail, she kicked my baby and I out leaving us displaced again.

When I look back over my life, I now realize that I was actually fighting to survive and even though there were many moments that brought me to my knees, I have always had hope and faith that things would get better for me. I just knew that with all the pain that life had served me, surely there had to be something good in store. I held out when I felt like giving up and I fought every single day. I believed that one day I would no longer have to struggle in order to survive, and that I would know what it was like to thrive instead.

I'm so grateful that I was able to eventually graduate from the struggle. Today, I'm on the other side of struggle although it was a long and hard road that came with many tough lessons. The resistance that I experienced along the way was strong. Even with so much potential as a young, fearless and ambitious teenager; the choices that I made in my adolescents have been the driving force of many of the obstacles I've had to overcome.

I was arrested for the first time at the age of nineteen years old and I received a different mugshot every year after that. I was arrested seven different times for various crimes ranging from theft, criminal damage to property, resisting arrest, violating probation and tampering with government records. I was nineteen years old selling weed and hard drugs during the day and clocking in as a stripper at night. I was young and wild, but even back then, I knew the importance of having multiple streams of income.

I struggled to discover my sense of self. Failure to love and value myself properly caused me to choose men who were toxic and abusive. I've always been a natural born hustler. If there was a way to make money, I was going to find it. The memories of my mother dressed in luxury clothing has always inspired me to make money so that I could dress good, even if I didn't feel that way.

I was a beautiful girl, but I didn't see myself that way. I had no confidence and I tolerated poor treatment from the men in my life. I gave myself to people who didn't deserve me and I tolerated things that no woman should ever have to put up with. By the time I gave birth to my second daughter, I was making even more money but dealing with more problems as a result of it. Even with a steadily increasing cash flow, I still felt trapped and even empty at times. It was like I was in a toxic cycle of going to jail, losing it all, then hustling to get it back, all while being disappointed and hurt by the people around me. I decided to give myself a fresh start, so I packed up my two daughters and we relocated from Illinois to Houston, Texas. I was running away from a very unhealthy relationship with my daughters father, and I was running away from the drama that I couldn't seem to break away from. I was tired and ready for a different life.

Raising two small children as a young single mother felt like I was carrying the weight of the world on my shoulders. On top of taking care of my children, I was the custodial caretaker of my brother who was diagnosed with cerebral palsy after being dropped on his head as a baby. His injury was the reason my biological mother lost custody of my siblings and I. Throughout the years, my father and I remained close, so when I relocated to Houston, he was there to help me move. Once we were settled in from the move, my father found work in a factory and he too decided to leave Illinois and relocate to Houston with us. Having my father join us in Houston provided me with some relief. He was able to help me out with my children and even split the cost of rent and other bills. Unfortunately, he ended up suffering from a stroke which left him temporarily incompetent. I then took on the responsibility of caring for him as he recovered.

During that time in my life, I was experiencing multiple transitions at once. Moving to a new city and trying to establish a business while balancing the responsibilities of caring for my children, my handicap brother and my temporarily disabled father. I gained employment working as a home health aide for my brother. I had been fired from multiple jobs. They would hire me, and then fire me once my background check came in. It was a season that tested me to my core, but things started to look up after I met David that day at the gas station. From the start, he would always encourage me to do and be better. He believed in me in a way that made me want to become a better version of myself. The right relationships are catalyst for growth. Not only did David come into my life and influence me to evolve, but I also met a woman who poured into me. She was a business woman who ran a local tax office. After we connected, I took interest in learning more about the tax filing process. I began working with her and she educated me on the tax filing and credit restoration business. I was a natural and we were experiencing a surplus in clientele. Due to the increase in demand for services, I decided to branch out and launch my own agency. My big city hustle gave me a huge advantage while working in the south. My experience, coupled with my ability to serve up southern hospitality proved to be a recipe for an increase in success.

When I originally launched my business, I was developing move-in packages for clients who had negative marks on their backgrounds that would prevent them from being approved for housing. Most of my clients were Houston's ballers and high rollers who wanted to secure luxury rentals despite having felony convictions or other derogatory marks on their credit profiles. Over the course of five years, I made nearly three million dollars securing housing for them by hiding evictions, broken leases and even felonies which would all guarantee a lease denial. I was making money on the front end and the back end by creating CPN profiles for them and then applying for and getting them approved for luxury rentals to accommodate their lifestyles.

I had an entire system including a team of employees who helped me to manage my highly successful operation. On one particular day, one of my clients was scheduled to sign their lease and move into their new high rise. My employee, who was also my cousin, would typically manage the lease signing and move in process. However, she was out of town on this particular day so I decided to use her ID and handle the move-in process myself. The leasing manager suspected fraud after looking at the submitted identification documents and determining that the photo did not appear to me. She had me wait in a room filling out additional documents as she alerted the authorities who were en route unbeknownst to me. I realized that something was wrong when I saw the police officers pull up. I was already on probation for two separate, yet similar charges. Prior to this incident. I was arrested for shoplifting, and I was involved in a traffic violation that resulted in my arrest. During both of my previous arrests, I was in possession of several credit cards with various names printed in on them. Knowing that getting in trouble again would be my third strike, I attempted to escape through the side door but was eventually apprehended. This was the last straw and the prosecutors were seeking prison time. When they couldn't charge me with fraud, they filed charges against me for tampering with government records. Technically, I had never committed fraud. I was hacking into the governments system and creating social security numbers. My crime was against the US government and they were malicious in their attempts to convict me.

David and I were at a point in our lives where we were exhausted from the high and lows of hustling. We were tired of taking turns in and out of jail. We had fallen in love and we wanted better for one another, ourselves and the family we were building together. After a year of dating, David proposed to me and we started planning the wedding of our dreams. Since I was out on bond, prosecutors were watching our every move as we were planning our wedding.

During a court hearing, the prosecutors went so far as to show images from our social media accounts in an attempt to label me as a flight risk. They knew we were planning to get married back home in Chicago and they decided to use our wedding as leverage to get me to take a plea. They would only allow me to travel to Chicago for my wedding if I agreed to a six-month prison sentence. I would also have to agree to turn myself in the day after the wedding. We had spent an elaborate amount of money on our wedding and we were prepared to host nearly two hundred close friends and family members. David originally didn't want me to take the plea, but I was unwilling to not go through with the wedding of my dreams with the love of my life. So, I decided to take the deal.

Our wedding was everything that I dreamed it would be. We were married at the same venue were former President Barack Obama and former First Lady Michelle Obama had been married. We even paid tribute to them by recreating their wedding photos. Our wedding day was full of pure bliss. We were surrounded by the love of all the people who meant the world do us. It was a true celebration of love. I didn't want the day to end; we were enjoying our ceremony so much, plus I knew that the next day I would be back in Texas preparing for prison.

When the time came, it felt like having a rug pulled from beneath me. I went from enjoying the best day of my life, to entering a season that would change my life forever.

That day was filled with *tears, fears and the hard truth* that if I didn't make a drastic change, I would be risking time away from my family again and I was no longer willing to do that.

PART THREE

SURVIVING WAS
THE ONLY OPTION

"David's Journey"

~~~~~~~~~~~~~~~~~~~~~~~~~~~~~~~~~~~~

"The genius thing that we
did was we didn't quit"

~Jay Z

I was chasing a check but trouble seemed to follow me. I grew up in a two-parent home. My parents were homeowners and serial entrepreneurs who owned and operated a grocery store, construction company and a liquor store. They were one of the first African Americans to own a liquor and grocery store in the late 70's. They were pillars within our family and community. If there was a family member who needed support or a place to live, they were always willing to open our home to those in need. They raised my brothers and I to value family, loyalty, hard work and hustle. My parents were firm with their rules, but they were also the parents that you could still talk to about anything. I was the youngest of seven children and although we had a strong family dynamic, we struggled in other ways.

Being raised in an environment where success was defined by money, lifestyle and materialism; my siblings and I were naturally attracted to the fast life. It was a proven and accessible way to get money fast.

In the inner city of Chicago, you had to be a ball player, drug dealer, gang member or rapper in order to "make it." My parents were a great example of success, but I was too ignorant then to respect the fact that anything worth having was worth the time it would require to build. My parents represented the process of success, but my adolescent mind desired immediate gratification. I wanted overnight success so I chose the promise of fast money through the streets.

My parents had always been such a good influence for me at home, but our environment outside of that, as well as its many negative influences had my attention. When you are raised in an environment consumed with hardship, violence, criminal behavior, grief and incarceration, it's easy to fall into the trap of thinking that life doesn't have more to offer you. The truth is, in order to break free from the trap, you will first have to break the chains in your mind. It took me a while to really understand this, but when I finally started to open my mind to the idea of a life of success that didn't include death or jail time, I started to see the world differently. I began to make decisions with my future in mind. I stopped taking the type of risks that could possibly jeopardize my ability to take care of and spend time with my family.

Being the youngest in the family, I naturally looked up to my older siblings. All of my older siblings sold drugs including my older sister who ended up going to prison for a drug offense.

Our neighborhood was filled with crime, social injustice and police brutality. I can remember a time when our home was raided by police and as a result of extreme police force, my mother's arm was broken. We were a good family in a bad environment and *surviving was the only option.*

When my brother "Boo" went to prison, I lost a role model. Even though he was in the streets, he was the person I would look to for guidance and direction.

Throughout my youth, I was active in sports. I was naturally athletic, so, I excelled in all the sports that I participated in. Basketball was my favorite. A great piece of advice that my brother Boo gave me was to choose one sport to focus on and to stick with it. I chose basketball and I became a high school star. I received basketball scholarships and I ended up signing to Iowa state. Unfortunately, because I didn't have patience and I didn't understand the power of trusting the process, I quit the program when the coaches attempted to "Red Shirt" me. This meant that I wouldn't start and would spend the first year on the bench.

When I left Iowa State, I decided to attend Texas College which was an HBCU in Tyler, Texas. Throughout my college career as Texas College, my focus was divided. I was at the top of my game while playing ball and selling drugs. College was supposed to be an outlet, and in many ways it was. I had one foot in the streets and the other on the court. One way or another, one of the two were going to bring me success. At least that's what I thought at the time.

It's funny how life works. You can think you've got it all figured out, and as soon as you start to believe that you finally got it together, life will throw you a curve ball. Like the night of my college graduation. While I was walking across the stage and celebrating success, my brother was murdered back home in Chicago. I can't imagine the strength my parents had to have in order to sit through my ceremony, smiling for me and knowing that they had just lost their older son. They put on a brave face because they didn't want to ruin my graduation with the news. They broke the news to me the next day and I remember feeling so numb. My parents pushed me to go to Mexico City in order to play basketball overseas. They didn't want me to come back to Chicago. I know they just didn't want to risk losing another child to the streets. Losing my brother was the first time that I experienced real grief. It was the first time that I lost someone so close to me. I mean, I had known people who had died, but losing my brother hurt more than anything I had experienced at that point in my life. My initial reaction was to seek revenge. In the streets, retaliation was a typical default response. The thing that caused me to reconsider, was the thought of my children having to visit me through a glass.

Prior to graduation, I had run into some trouble but by the grace of God I was able to escape hard jail time.

To be honest, God's grace has carried me a long way. When I was 22 years old and in college, I was facing time for my alleged involvement in a murder. I wasn't the shooter but I was in the car at the time of the crime.

There was an incident where my friends brother was murdered. Shortly after that, the person who killed him was also murdered. The feds believed that his homicide was a murder for hire plot with revenge as the motive. My coach took the initiative to speak up on my behalf and provided insight on my character as a student athlete. My coach was someone I respected.

He was like my father away from home. He was an upright man who would take our basketball team to church on Sunday's. He was a positive influence in my life and he had a way of keeping me level-headed. Eventually with no evidence and with the support of my coach, the feds eventually moved on and I was able to escape further investigation. My friend wasn't as fortunate. He was charged and sentenced to fifty-three years in federal prison.

That entire ordeal was a close call and an eye opener. It shook me up and helped me to really see what I had on the line. It also made me realize that I had people in my corner who really did want to see me win.

I was like the Michael Jordan of my neighborhood. I had a reputation for winning and the people around me always expected me to win. So, I always carried some degree of pressure to not let them down.

I left Mexico City after six months and I moved to Texas City. I gained employment working at a plant while also playing semi-pro basketball for the Lake Jackson Lakers. I removed myself from gang violence, but I was still selling drugs until I was pulled over for a traffic violation in St. Louis. I was caught with one hundred and fifty pounds of marijuana plus seventy-five thousand dollars in cash. I was arrested and locked up in St. Louis for two months. The disappointing thing about that day, was the fact that I was supposed to be on a flight to Chicago to try out for the Chicago Bulls. I remember getting a gut feeling to go straight to the airport, but I ignored it. Dismissing my intuition cost me the opportunity to play in the NBA. Not only did I miss out on the Chicago tryout, but all of my other tryouts were cancelled as well. I was scheduled to try-out for the Los Angeles Lakers and the Minnesota Timberwolves in the coming weeks. Once I received bail, I bonded out on a two hundred- and fifty-thousand-dollar bond.

After being released, things seemed to go from bad to worst. When I bonded out, the conditions of my release required me to relocate to Chicago for the duration of my two-year probation sentence.

In Chicago, I was back in the same environment that placed me in proximity of gang violence, drugs and other street traps. Since everyone back home held an expectation for me to win, of course I kept up my appearance. I was flashy, and living fast. The drug money provided me with the resources to live a good life, so I started selling more drugs so that I could make even more money. Afterall, success to me at the time was about having enough money to spend to look rich. I was making money fast, and spending it even faster.

In 2011, I violated my probation by getting caught with a half-pound of marijuana. My probation was extended and I was stuck in Chicago longer. I tried to get my probation transferred to Texas but the judge denied my request.

The inner city of Chicago can be very dangerous. In 2013, my sister and I were robbed in her home after being targeted in a corner store. My sister needed to grab some items from the corner store so I walked with her to the store. While paying for the items, there was a guy in the store watching us and trying to engage in small talk. He complimented my shoes, and I'm sure he noticed the large amount of cash I pulled from my pocket to pay for my sisters items. I got a bad vibe from the guy and kept the conversation short with him. Once we arrived to my sisters building, the same guy from the grocery store approached us from behind at gunpoint. He put his gun to my head, took my watch, and one of my earrings. I could see him trembling and I knew he was nervous. My first instinct was to fight him off, but I didn't want to risk my sister getting shot in the crossfire, so, I gave him whatever he asked for.

My cousins were already on the way to my sister's house to pick me up, they arrived while the robbery was in progress. The robbery quickly turned into a shoot-out once my cousins pulled up.

That night, so many things could have gone wrong but again, God's grace covered my sister, my cousins and I. My nephew had just received a forty-three-year sentence in a federal drug case and

I didn't want to see anymore loved ones lose their lives to gun violence or the penitentiary.

It was all becoming so redundant but I was slowly getting more and more fed up with the street life.

I was robbed again, but this time it was by people who were close to me. People who I believed were for me. When I was violated in such a way by someone I knew, it made me realize that the game had changed, and no 'one was playing by the rules. It used to be a street code violation for people in your camp to cross you, but the streets didn't value loyalty the way they used to.

The combination of betrayal on top of my wife's prison sentence was just enough to finally make me choose to play the game of life in a more legit way. I was tired of the streets and it was clear that we needed to do things differently.

PART FOUR

THE SHIFT

"Surviving The Breaking Point"

ჟჟჟჟჟჟჟჟჟჟჟჟჟჟჟჟჟჟჟჟჟჟჟჟჟჟჟჟ

"Growth doesn't happen by chance;

It happens by change"

~Anonymous

Perhaps we were chasing the right things but for the wrong reasons. Like most people who were fighting to survive the struggle, we had dreams of getting rich. We wanted the nice cars, expensive clothes, lavish parties and international vacations. We were using our skills to get the things we wanted in life, but because we hadn't evolved mentally, we couldn't see how we could apply our street hustling skills to legitimate businesses. Prison changed that for me. For David, it was the frustration of navigating a series of loss, betrayal and one too many court appearances. The streets cost us too much and we could no longer afford to live our lives the same way.

When I was released from prison, we were facing eviction and our vehicles were up for repossession. Deciding to go legit required that we shift from fast money to strategic revenue. It wasn't a smooth transition; we would have to build from the bottom up all over again. Before we started earning millions of dollars in our legitimate business ventures, we would first lose it all. The thing about being a true hustler is that you have the will power and resilience to bounce back from every loss.

It took time, strategy, mentorship, a shift in perspective, prayer, faith, determination, healing inner wounds and nurturing positive relationships to finally begin to experience transformation. We started making decisions with our children and their futures in mind. We could no longer be reckless, we now had to move with discernment, discretion and discipline.

We started focusing on the values, business practices and biblical principles that we were both exposed to early on in our lives. My grandparents led a church and they made sure that I knew the word. I didn't appreciate it when I was younger. I rebelled against them in my teen years, but as an adult I found myself leaning onto their wisdom.

It was their faith inspired wisdom as well as prayer that comforted me in the jail cell. When I felt like I was suffocating, I had to remember what God's word said. I would tell myself not to worry, because Gods promises for my life were real.

We wanted to share our stories, because too often people celebrate your winning season without understanding what you endured in order to survive your struggle season. There are so many men and women today who get up every day and take penitentiary chances. Whether their motivation is being able to afford materialism, or they are hustling for a way out of the hood, the end result is often the same. Without a real plan, access to transformational information and the willingness to stretch yourself, dreams are often interrupted by the harsh reality of violence, incarceration or senseless casualties. When we were able to break into a new way of living, it was important that we helped others to do the same. We knew too well the pain of misguided decisions and misaligned ambition. Without real role models, too many of us go down a path of destruction. We either don't know any better or we refuse to do better.

We wanted to break the cycle by showing others another way to "make it." We were no longer hustling for labels; we were grinding to build a legacy. We wanted to establish the type of wealth that our children and grandchildren would benefit from.

It all started from a changed and committed mind. I told myself that once I was released, I would invest in my personal development. I also wanted to connect with other women who were focused on building wealth and were on a positive path. I would reach out to people who were where I wanted to be. I wasn't shy about asking for help. I wasn't satisfied with what I didn't know, if I didn't have an answer, I would find someone who did. I wasn't going back to prison so I had to apply pressure to the old version of who I was.

My experience as a drug dealer gave me the sales and distribution skills that I utilize in my business to gain more clients and revenue today. David's experience in a gang taught him organizational structure, operations and logistics. We doubled down and started leveraging all of our combined skills, resources, connections, ideas and experiences. It's funny how we benefit from both the good and the bad things in our lives when we are gracious enough to express gratitude for the good things and wise enough to learn from the bad things.

When I work with women, I hear a lot of them mention how much they hate their jobs and how they can't wait to quit and start their own business. I always encourage them to proceed with wisdom and caution. Many times I find that they are overlooking all of the benefits that their current job has to offer. Many companies offer trainings, certification resources to increase personal development, time management and other organizational and managerial tools. I often tell women to take a deeper look at their employment benefits in order to fully assess the value of their position. Too many people are ready to walk away from situations prematurely because they don't have an eye for opportunity. It's going to be really hard to be a successful entrepreneur, if you are a short-sighted employee. You will be surprised at how much of what you learn along the way is used to catapult you to success. Take nothing for granted and treat every opportunity like it could be the one that changes your life for good, because the truth is, it can.

Our businesses are highly successful in large part today because of what we learned about sales, team building, supply and demand trends, plus scalability while in the streets. Committing crimes was not the best use of our energy, time or talent, however, we had not yet developed a vision bigger for ourselves.

Never underestimate the power of your current position. Where you are now counts. You may not be exactly where you want to be but, you are in the process of progress.

Collectively, we are proof that you can start from the bottom, be born into poverty, break away from gang violence, overcome incarceration, and still fall in love, establish an unbreakable bond, build a family and generate wealth. With the proper mindset, the right people in your corner, focus, strategy and determination, you can redesign your entire life. We did it and you deserve a shot at living the life of your dreams too.

Don't settle for a life that limits you. Believe in yourself and your potential. Don't ever believe that you aren't capable, worthy or deserving of experiencing the good that life has to offer. I challenge you to see yourself in a bigger way. Having a vision for a new life was key for us. We saw a different life and we believed that we had what it would take to it materialize authentic success in our lives.

We've lost way too many of our loved to gun violence, jail, mental illness and abuse. When we decide to live, think, believe and behave in a different way, we begin to break the chains that keep us and the people we're connected to stuck. That's why your connections are so important. The people attached to you either drain you or spark you. They pull you closer to your destiny or they distract and detour you from it, so choose wisely.

Being surrounded by the right influences can change the trajectory of your life in a positive way. When you decide to grow, you will also need to change your environment. This is not limited to your physical location. You will also need to pay attention to what you consume, what you listen to and the type of people you engage with. In order to experience a drastically different life, you must make drastic changes and stick with them.

Today we own and operate several six and seven figure companies. We are serial entrepreneurs who are passionate about generating wealth, acquiring assets and maintaining healthy credit while empowering our community to do the same.

The odds were stacked against us and we faced several lessons that we had to learn from along the way, but we made it out and you can to. You just have to believe that its possible, know that you deserve it and be willing to work towards it.

PART FIVE

THE LESSONS THAT COME BEFORE LEGACY

"You can never grow from
what you refuse to learn from"
~Anonymous

Before we were able to manage six and seven figure revenue streams, we had to develop and implement effective revenue generating strategies. Before we were able to build a healthy and loving marriage, we had to endure separation and isolation that tested the strength of our bond. Having a vision for our future expanded our minds. We saw more for ourselves and we were inspired to create a plan to achieve our goals.

Marriage is one of the most important partnerships that you can have. It teaches you the power of balancing strengths, working together, combining effort and establishing win-win outcomes. Just like business, marriage should consist of both parties having their needs and desires met. A healthy partnership is one where benefits are distributed among those involved proportionately. Couples who share common goals, values, and interests, and are able to work together efficiently are able to achieve more.

Monogamy and Loyalty are not a lost art although our society glamourizes dysfunction and broken family dynamics. Contrary to popular culture, having someone to build with who also influences you to become a better version of yourself is the real bag.

There are people in this world who genuinely want to see you win and will support you. Break out of your normal routine, disrupt your pattern of thinking and get out and find your tribe. There is only so much you can do alone. There's an African Proverb that says, "If you want to go fast, go alone. But if you want to go far, take the right people." I would even take it further to add, not only do you need the right people, you need an inspired plan, a positive mindset and the ability to focus all the way to the finish line.

Our love story and our journey towards legacy was a road less traveled, but through it all we stayed committed to one another and the future that we believed in. We turned our losses into lessons, and our pain into blessings.

We wrote this book, not just to inspire total life transformation, but to highlight the importance of black love and the representation of legitimate success. We want to normalize passing down wealth in our families instead of trauma and debt. When we heal from the brokenness and broken mindset of our pasts, we create room in our lives for new and exciting things to happen for us.

Today we are empowering thousands of people with the tools to gain financial health through our "Empire You" credit repair agency, traveling the world and creating memories as a family, while normalizing being young, black and rich. We hope that our story inspires redemption, resilience, elevation and transformation. May you find and fall madly in love with someone you can bond and build with. Do it for the culture. Do it for your legacy. Do it for all of those who you know and love who won't ever get the chance to do it. Do it for your children. Do it for future generations. Do it because you believe that you can rise higher; may you remain committed, focused, coachable, resilient and prayerful as you are working towards your dreams and *chasing the empire.*

CHASING THE EMPIRE
AFFIRMATIONS

*Above all, love each other deeply, because love
covers over a multitude of sins.*

1 Peter 4:8

LOVE AFFIRMATIONS

I am lovable even when someone lacks the ability to love me properly.

I don't have to settle for a love that hurts, true love is available to me and it's worth the wait.

When I love myself first, I treat others how to love me in return.

I am allowed to walk away from relationships that disrupt my peace.

I believe in love and I know that I am deserving of it even if I've been hurt in the past.

I heal from past trauma because I don't want my broken pieces to sabotage my ability to make a healthy attachment.

I am allowed to choose myself and I'm empowered to make decisions that are best for me.

In order to earn six and seven figures, you will need to examine your relationship with money. As you transition from a poverty mindset towards an abundant mindset; it's important that you shift your beliefs about money and your ability to earn it, manage it and maximize it. You will need to believe that you are capable, deserving and equipped to create lucrative revenue streams.

Here are some Money Affirmations to help you reframe your beliefs about money.

MONEY AFFIRMATIONS

Money comes to me freely and effortlessly every day.

I am a multi-millionaire and I successfully manage multiple streams of income.

I work smarter not harder. I know that I don't have to burn out in order to be successful.

I am capable and deserving of building wealth.

I am creative, skilled, strategic and hard working. I recognize opportunities and when there are none, I create them.

I have the capacity to manage, 6, 7 and 8 figure businesses,

I am focused and I work my plan.

I am clear about my goals and I make wise decisions to achieve them.

I employ discernment in my decision-making process and I surround myself with people who add value to my life.

I influence growth, power and I am a positive influence.

I believe God's promises for my life and I know that he has given me the power to get wealth.

I am a wealth magnet.

I will never be broke another day in my life.

I am powerful.

I am chosen by God.

I am protected by God.

I celebrate myself daily because I am grateful for even the small things.

Leaving a legacy will require that you create something that will outlive you. That can be through estate, investments, property or other assets. When our children inherit opportunities, they are able to build upon what we leave behind for them. Legacy requires that you have a vision for the future that benefits future generations. As we transition from a survival mindset, having positive affirmations is a true asset.

LEGACY AFFIRMATIONS

I have a vision that creates opportunities for myself and others.

When I win, I give others an opportunity to win as well.

Giving back is a true reflection of success.

I am creating new ways of thinking, living and thriving in my family.

I am breaking chains and creating new habits.

I learn from my past but I focus on my future.

I won't take short cuts in life. I realize that having a solid foundation is key for sustainability and massive growth.

I can do great things the right way.

I never take my imagination for granted. I know that my mind holds million-dollar ideas.

I don't ignore my intuition, I know that my gut feelings are there to guide me towards a happy, healthy and prosperous future.

I eliminate distractions so that I can focus on opportunities.

I know that God has a plan for my life, so I trust Him even when things don't seem to be going my way.

When things appear to be falling apart, they could actually be coming together.

I separate from bad influences and I choose good people who are good for my growth.

I know that having a plan and sticking with it can completely change my life.

I know that proper preparation prevents piss poor performance so I practice and plan to win.

I guard my mind and protect my peace. I know that I am only as strong as my thoughts.

I dismiss negative thoughts and I take charge of my mind.

I prioritize reading, I know that readers are leaders.

Dear Mama,

I never got the chance to build a relationship with my mother. I always wondered what life would have been like if she had not had her life stripped away from her. I missed out many intimate moments and conversations with my mother. So, as part of my healing process, I wrote a heartfelt letter to her. I always felt the need to express my sentiments and writing this letter gave me the opportunity to release the thoughts and emotions that I carried throughout my childhood and early adulthood.

Letter to my mother

Dear Mama,

"I am grateful that you tried your best. I am hopeful that I will continue to live out your legacy and continue breaking the curses that are on our family. I've come to realize that your death did not happen to me, but it happened for me. I think differently now. I make better decisions now because of my fear of not being around for my children. I do better because I can't imagine leaving my children and not leaving behind anything for them.

I am no longer afraid. I know that because of my circumstances, I can create change to encourage a better outcome for my children, my family and my community.

Mama. I want you to know that I've been helping people all over the world to also change their circumstances so that they too can leave a legacy. I can finally see mom,

My eyes were so blinded, I thought I was a victim for so many years. I am a leader and I have limitless potential. There is nothing that I cannot do. My trauma has turned into triumph and I am forever grateful. Thank you for being who you were. Our family tragedy was hard and it disrupted our family dynamic, but it gave me an opportunity to grow and learn from my dad and grandparents who instilled faith into me. Their biblical teachings saved my life and I will be forever changed by the word. God's promises will reign over my family. Thank you for bringing me into this world. I survived…. And now I get to thrive….This is my Empire.

My Mother the Chain Breaker

"Letter from our oldest daughter Jaria,"

Watching my mother build her legacy is very inspiring to me. I'm her first born and I've been able to witness her endure trials and experience triumph. I'm so proud to be able to one day carry the torch and run my parent's business. I'm learning so much as I watch them build and Its my honor to continue to build upon and add to families empire.

ABOUT THE AUTHORS

David and Jessica Martin are serial entrepreneurs. They Co-operate "Empire You LLC" a multi-million-dollar credit repair company in Houston Texas and DR Martin

Transport LLC, a highly successful, family owned and operated trucking company in the Greater Texas area. They also own a tax filing firm through the IRS' E-Tax firms. Through philanthropic contribution, they educ ate and empower their community by providing access to credit repair and wealth building resources.

Connect with David and Jessica Martin:

The Empire Planner is for every budding entrepreneur and dreamer who desires to build their empire from the ground up. This planner focuses on starting at working for someone else to working for yourself. It takes the lessons that Jessica Martin used in order to build the business empire she has built today. If you're ready to invest in your future, this is the planner to help you layout your empire.

https://shopempireplanner.com

Learn more about how we help individuals start, build, scale and grow trucking businesses.

https://www.thetruckstart.com

Empire Tax Firms

We provide tax preparation services online and in office for W2 employees and small business owners.

https://etaxfirms.com

Jessica & Jessica's Mom

Bachelorette Party Las Vegas 2017

At the South Shore Cultural Center:

We imitated Barrack and Michelle Obama on their wedding day

Wedding Day 7/16/2017

Wedding July 16, 2017

Jessica's Mom

Engagement Party: David & Friends

David martin enjoying himself with his two brothers Sean

& James

Jessica's Mom, and friends

Jessica's Mom: Ilean

Jessica's Dad: Johnnie

Jessica's siblings: Jonathan, Jona, & Jessica

Engagement Party 7/17/2016

Engagement Party 7/17/2016

The theme of our wedding was on the run, and we made our bachelorette shirts each have a crime.

Christmas in Dubai 2021, after we successfully opened 4

businesses; enjoying our life freely and legally!

Our Wedding Day, July 17, 2017

Picture of Jessica Martin's mom and sisters

Our wedding day July 2017 and in 24 hours I would be

turning myself into custody.

Enjoying our engagement party July 2016, at this time we were selling drugs and living in the fast lane.

Plane State Jail 10/2017, one of my first visits I got to see my family after 3 months.

Husband & Wife celebrate adding an 18-Wheeler to their transportation company!

1,901 likes

blackwealthmvmnt S/O to This King & His Queen, they just added truck #5 to their business without using any of their own money #BlackExcellence 👊

👑👸 @empireu_credit

We went viral from our trucking company and adding to

our fleet.

When we were dealing heavy drugs and dealing with bags of

100s and 1000s of dollars at a time.

Me at sixteen years old & my first daughter

We now open up businesses for our family members and

help them with their goals.

We're able to fly private now and really live the life of our

dreams.

The kids Christmas 2020, the holidays are much different

When we purchased our first home. It's now worth a million

dollars in 2020. (5 Bedrooms, 5 Bathrooms & 5,000 Square

Feet)

January 2021: We won millionaire club award for our credit repair company surpassing a million dollars in sales.

James & Patricia Martin

(David's Parents)

James Martin Jr & Cindy Martin

(Brother & Wife)

Christmas in Dubai with our children

CPSIA information can be obtained
at www.ICGtesting.com
Printed in the USA
LVHW061742190922
728753LV00003B/27